I0797620

INSIDE THE NFL

GREEN BAY PACKERS

by Charlie Beattie

An imprint of Abdo Publishing
abdobooks.com

ABDOBOOKS.COM

Published by Abdo Publishing, a division of ABDO, PO Box 398166, Minneapolis, Minnesota 55439.

Printed in China.
052025
092025

Cover Photos: John Fisher/Getty Images Sport/Getty Images (Jordan Love); Focus on Sport/Getty Images (Bart Starr)
Interior Photos: Stacy Revere/Getty Images Sport/Getty Images, 4–5, 57; Joe Robbins/AP Images, 6; Dustin Bradford/Getty Images Sport/Getty Images, 7, 63; Patrick McDermott/Getty Images Sport/Getty Images, 8; Cooper Neill/Getty Images Sport/Getty Images, 9; Abdo Publishing, 10–11, 58; AP Images, 12–13, 14, 20, 33, 60 (bottom left), 60 (bottom right); Ed Maloney/AP Images, 15; Bettmann/Getty Images, 16, 18, 19, 21; Sporting News/Getty Images, 17; Tony Tomsic/AP Images, 22–23, 29, 30, 34, 61 (bottom left); Ross Lewis/Getty Images Sport/Getty Images, 24; Focus on Sport/Getty Images, 25, 31, 36–37, 60 (top); Focus on Sport/Getty Images Sport/Getty Images, 26, 35; Matt Patterson/AP Images, 28; Charles Krupa/AP Images, 38; Jim Slosiarek/Racine Journal Times/AP Images, 39, 61 (top left); David Stluka/AP Images, 40, 50; Mark Duncan/AP Images, 41; Todd Ponath/AP Images, 42; Tom DiPace/AP Images, 43, 45; Jeff Haynes/AP Images for Panini/AP Images, 46–47, 61 (top right); Wesley Hitt/Getty Images Sport/Getty Images, 48; Dilip Vishwanat/Getty Images Sport/Getty Images, 49; Kevin C. Cox/Getty Images Sport/Getty Images, 51; Brian Bahr/Allsport/Getty Images Sport/Getty Images, 52; Jonathan Daniel/Getty Images Sport/Getty Images, 53; Rob Tringali/SportsChrome/Getty Images, 54, 61 (bottom right); Rick Scuteri/AP Images, 55; Morry Gash/AP Images, 56; Michael Owens/Getty Images Sport/Getty Images, 59

Editor: Chrös McDougall
Series Designer: Laura Graphenteen
Production Designer: Ryan Gale

Library of Congress Control Number: 2024948497

Publisher's Cataloging-in-Publication Data

Names: Beattie, Charlie, author.
Title: Green Bay Packers / by Charlie Beattie
Description: Minneapolis, Minnesota: Abdo Publishing, 2026 | Series: Inside the NFL | Includes online resources and index.
Identifiers: ISBN 9781098296735 (lib. bdg.) | ISBN 9798384919254 (ebook)
Subjects: LCSH: Green Bay Packers (Football team)--Juvenile literature. | National Football League--Juvenile literature. | Football teams--Juvenile literature. | American football--Juvenile literature.
Classification: DDC 796.33264--dc23

CONTENTS

Packers quarterback Jordan Love looks to throw against the Los Angeles Chargers during their 2023 game.

CHAPTER 1

LOVE'S LATE WINNER

JORDAN LOVE LOOKED RELAXED AND CONFIDENT AS HE AWAITED THE shotgun snap. His cool nature was a big contrast from the huge moment he was facing. It was Week 11 of the 2023 National Football League (NFL) season. Love's Green Bay Packers trailed the Los Angeles Chargers 20–16. And with less than three minutes to go, the Packers were running out of time. A crowd of more than 77,000 fans at Green Bay's Lambeau Field looked on in anticipation. Everyone was hoping for the young quarterback to come through.

Love was in his first year as a starter for one of the NFL's most storied teams. Quarterbacking Green Bay was a huge honor but also a huge responsibility. The passionate fans of the league's smallest city were used to winning, and they were used to stars under center, too.

Brett Favre, *left*, threw 442 touchdowns in 16 seasons with the Packers. Aaron Rodgers, *right*, played 18 seasons for the team and threw 475 touchdowns.

CRADLE OF QUARTERBACKS

Finding star quarterbacks in the NFL is difficult. Any team is lucky to land a passer who can lead the way on the field for more than a decade. But entering the 2023 season, Packers fans had been treated to nearly 30 years of stellar passing.

The run started with Brett Favre, whose swashbuckling style of play and rocket arm thrilled fans starting in 1992. It continued with Aaron Rodgers, who took over as the starter in 2008. Rodgers remained one of the NFL's best players in 2020 when Green Bay's front office shocked the league by picking Love in the first round of that year's draft. Observers were surprised the team would spend such a high pick on a player who wouldn't get on the field right away. But the Packers didn't want to pass up a potential future star.

Love watched from the sideline for his first three years. When Rodgers moved on before the 2023 season, Love was set to take over. But he had played so little that few knew whether he was ready to carry on the team's proud tradition.

Through the first nine games of the season, the results weren't promising. Green Bay entered its game against the Chargers with a 3-6 record. Another loss would almost certainly knock the Packers out of contention for a playoff spot.

RIGHT ON TARGET

With the Packers down late, Love knew it was his time to shine. "Go finish. Go compete. And go be great," he told himself. Love and the Packers faced second-and-eight at the Los Angeles 24 with 2:38 left in the game. As Love dropped back, he noticed receiver Romeo Doubs streaking down the left sideline. Doubs had a step on his defender as he crossed into the end zone. But Love still needed his pass to be perfect. If he drifted the ball too deep or too wide, the pass would lead Doubs out of bounds.

Entering the game against the Chargers, Love had thrown 14 touchdown passes and 10 interceptions in nine games in 2023.

Packers wide receiver Romeo Doubs leaps to grab the game-winning touchdown against the Chargers.

With time to throw, Love settled himself and lofted a perfect strike. A defender reached out to try to knock the ball away. It was no use. Doubs leaped high in the air to pull the ball in. He secured the catch while tumbling down in the end zone for the go-ahead score.

That type of pass was exactly what Packers fans were hoping to see from their starting quarterback. It also came in the perfect situation. The touchdown put Green Bay up 23–20 with 2:33 left. The Packers' defense then snuffed out two Chargers drives to secure the season-saving victory.

The Packers had high hopes for Love. He lived up to them against the Chargers, throwing for more than 300 yards for the first time in his young career. And Love continued to play like a star after that, leading Green Bay to six victories in the team's final eight games. Love's performance not only led the Packers back to the playoffs but also showed he had the potential to be the next great star to wear the team's famous uniform.

STICKING WITH LOVE

The Packers were so impressed with Jordan Love's play in 2023 that they awarded him a rich new contract after the season. The team signed Love to a new four-year contract worth $220 million. At the time, Love's $55 million annual salary was tied for the highest in the league with two other star quarterbacks.

Jordan Love

NFL TEAMS MAP

NFC EAST

-  DALLAS COWBOYS
- 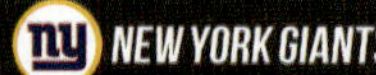 NEW YORK GIANTS
-  PHILADELPHIA EAGLES
-  WASHINGTON COMMANDERS

NFC WEST

-  ARIZONA CARDINALS
-  LOS ANGELES RAMS
-  SAN FRANCISCO 49ERS
-  SEATTLE SEAHAWKS

NFC NORTH

-  CHICAGO BEARS
-  DETROIT LIONS
-  GREEN BAY PACKERS
-  MINNESOTA VIKINGS

NFC SOUTH

-  ATLANTA FALCONS
-  CAROLINA PANTHERS
-  NEW ORLEANS SAINTS
-  TAMPA BAY BUCCANEERS

AFC

AFC EAST

- BUFFALO BILLS
- MIAMI DOLPHINS
- NEW ENGLAND PATRIOTS
- NEW YORK JETS

AFC WEST

- DENVER BRONCOS
- KANSAS CITY CHIEFS
- LAS VEGAS RAIDERS
- LOS ANGELES CHARGERS

AFC NORTH

- BALTIMORE RAVENS
- CINCINNATI BENGALS
- CLEVELAND BROWNS
- PITTSBURGH STEELERS

AFC SOUTH

- HOUSTON TEXANS
- INDIANAPOLIS COLTS
- JACKSONVILLE JAGUARS
- TENNESSEE TITANS

Curly Lambeau, *center*, played for the Packers until 1926 in addition to owning the team.

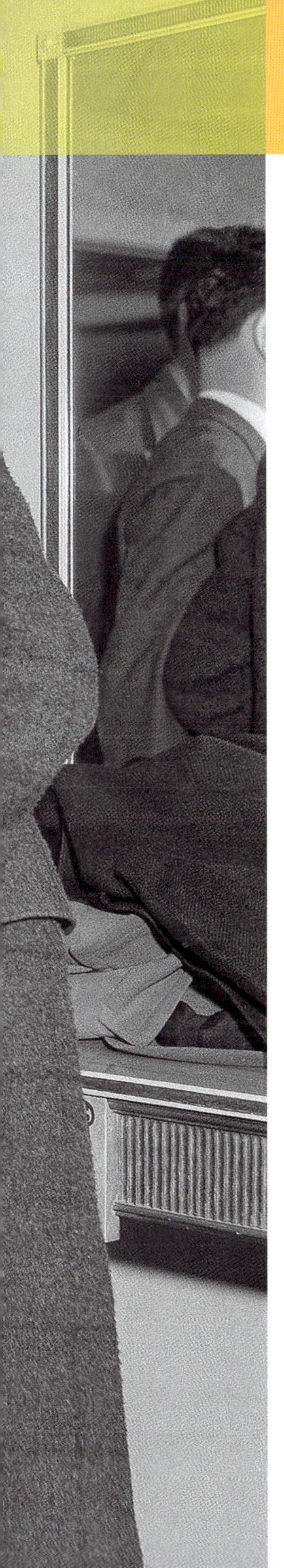

CHAPTER 2

THE PACKING COMPANY

In 1919, Curly Lambeau quit the football team at the University of Notre Dame and moved back to his hometown of Green Bay, Wisconsin. Lambeau took a job producing canned food at the Indian Packing Company. He also joined forces with local newspaperman George Whitney Calhoun to start a community football team, which Lambeau coached and played for. Taking a $500 donation from his company, Lambeau bought jerseys for the team. Soon after, Calhoun's newspaper, the *Green Bay Press-Gazette*, began referring to the team as "the Packers."

Professional football was still in its infancy. Originally, the Packers played only against other teams in the area. But Calhoun's constant hype in the *Press-Gazette* boosted the Packers' reputation. This helped them get the attention

The Packers, *in light uniforms*, take on the New York Giants in a game during the 1920s.

of the new American Professional Football Association (APFA). Founded in 1920, the APFA welcomed the Packers for its second season in 1921, even though Green Bay was much smaller than the other cities in the league. One year later, the APFA changed its name to the NFL.

SCANDAL AND REBIRTH

Today, the Packers are celebrated as one of the NFL's oldest and most successful teams. Yet the team almost didn't last beyond its first few seasons. In football's early days, players joined and left teams all the time during the season. Late in 1921, Lambeau's Packers needed some help for an exhibition against a team from Racine, Wisconsin. Green Bay signed three players from Notre Dame's roster.

At the time, college players were not allowed to take part in professional sports, or else they'd lose their amateur eligibility. To hide the amateurs, the Packers registered the trio under fake names. But when the team's deception was discovered, the Packers were booted from the NFL.

The ban didn't last long. Brothers J. Emmett and John Clair, who had supported the team early on, agreed to leave. Soon after, Lambeau paid a fine, and the NFL reinstated the Packers in time for the 1922 season. But the team's future looked bleak. The Packers were losing money. Bad weather didn't help. A handful of storms late in the season in 1922 kept fans away. Without more investment, the team was in danger of folding.

THE WHISTLEBLOWER

The Packers' illegal-players scandal of 1922 helped create a lasting rivalry. George Halas, head coach of the Chicago Bears, told the NFL the Packers were using college players. Halas actually helped Curly Lambeau get back into the league a year later. However, many fans of both teams point to that moment as the start of one of the NFL's most storied rivalries. Today, the Packers and Bears still play two heated games each season.

George Halas, *left*, and Curly Lambeau coached against each other for nearly three decades.

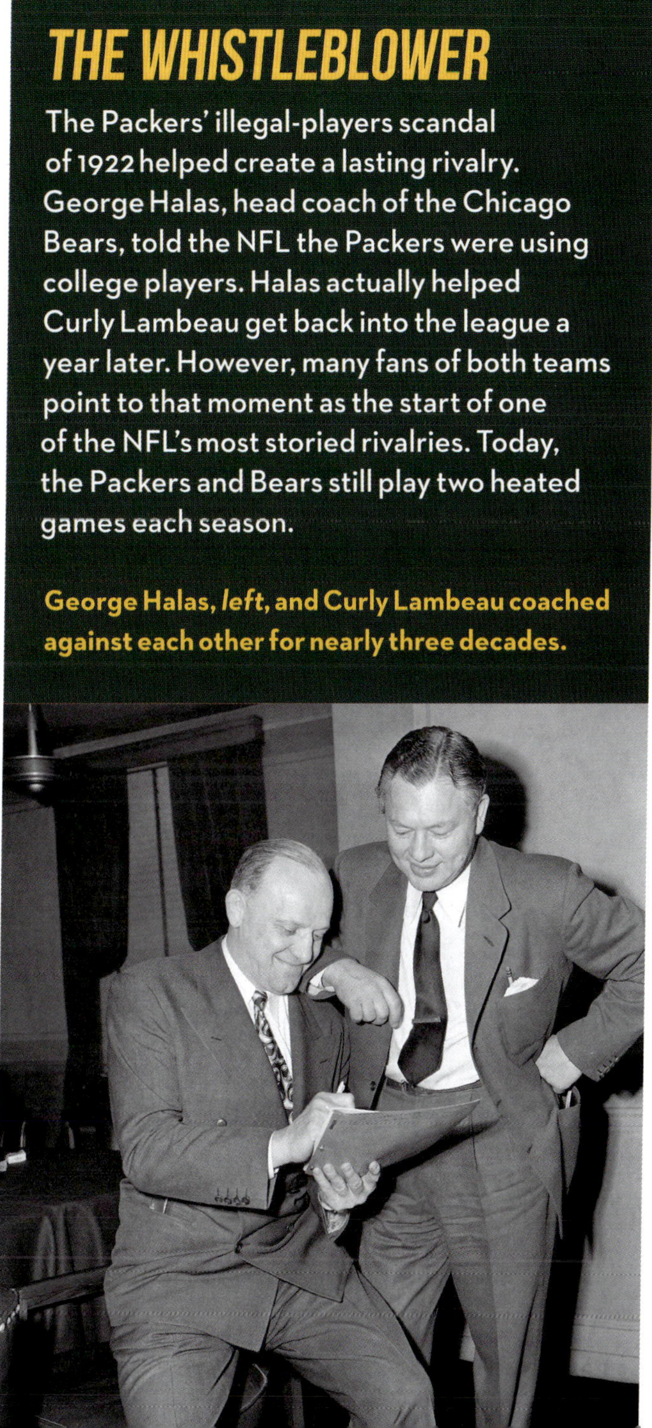

COMMUNITY CHAMPIONS

To save the team, four local businessmen agreed to cover Lambeau's debt. Then the five men came up with an idea. They issued stock in the team.

That way, any fan could buy a small piece of the Packers. Instead of a handful of private owners, the team would be owned by the public. Thousands of fans chipped in and saved the Packers. That idea is still used today. The Packers are the only NFL team owned by public shareholders.

With the team's finances secure, Lambeau turned his attention to building a winner. The Packers had winning records for the rest of the decade. And in 1929, Lambeau built his first championship team. The coach had signed three star players before the season. Cal Hubbard and Mike Michalske were standout linemen on both sides of the ball. Running behind them on offense was a speedy back who was born John Victor McNally. But in 1922, after seeing a movie poster for a film called *Blood and Sand*, McNally decided to change his name. By the time he arrived in Green Bay, he was Johnny Blood.

The team finished 12–0–1 in 1929 and allowed just 22 points all season. With no playoffs at the time, the Packers clinched their first NFL championship by boasting the league's best record.

Lineman Cal Hubbard asked to be traded from the New York Giants to the Packers because he liked the small-town feel of Green Bay.

Halfback Johnny Blood was inducted into the Pro Football Hall of Fame in 1963.

Behind Blood, Hubbard, Michalske, and a handful of other stars, Lambeau's Packers won titles again in 1930 and 1931. In that span, Lambeau's men lost only five games. A decade after nearly failing, the Packers were the NFL's first dynasty.

HERBER TO HUTSON

Most teams kept the ball on the ground in football's early days. But in the 1930s, the passing game became much more of a weapon. And Lambeau's Packers led the revolution.

Quarterback Arnie "Flash" Herber grew up in Green Bay and played high school football at Green Bay West, where the Packers held their summer training camps. Lambeau gave the 20-year-old a tryout in 1930, and Herber soon became perhaps the league's best passer.

Herber led the NFL in passing yards and touchdown passes in 1932, the first year the league began keeping those statistics.

Arnie Herber grew up selling programs at Packers games before becoming the team's record-setting quarterback in the 1930s.

He led the league again in 1934. Then, in 1935, the Packers signed a receiver who truly turned their passing game into a juggernaut.

While Herber had the strong arm, Don Hutson turned receiving into an art form. "The Alabama Antelope" created several patterns that became staples of the passing game, including the buttonhook and the hook-and-go. Hutson ran those routes to perfection. Defenders struggled to keep up with his speed and shifty moves. Former coach Clark Shaughnessy once said, "No one but Superman could perform the feats Don Hutson has performed in catching passes."

"NO ONE BUT SUPERMAN COULD PERFORM THE FEATS DON HUTSON HAS PERFORMED IN CATCHING PASSES."

—CLARK SHAUGHNESSY

Green Bay's exceptional "Herber to Hutson" combination led to big wins. In 1933, the league introduced a championship game. Three years later, in 1936, the Packers posted the league's best record at 10-1-1 to earn a spot in the NFL Championship Game. Less than three minutes into the game against Boston, Herber took a snap at the Boston 48-yard line. Hutson broke down the field, and the quarterback threw a bomb to his receiver for a touchdown. Herber threw another touchdown pass in the third quarter, and the Packers won 21-6.

The Packers returned to the NFL Championship Game in 1939. This time, the New York Giants were able to shut down Hutson. But the Packers' defense stifled New York's offense completely. Herber and tailback Cecil Isbell each threw a touchdown pass, and Green Bay intercepted the Giants six times, in a 27–0 win.

END OF AN ERA

Herber played just one more season in Green Bay. Over his 11 seasons with the team, the Packers posted only one losing record. Many considered him to be the league's top passer at the time.

The Packers signed wide receiver Don Hutson out of the University of Alabama in 1935.

Behind Hutson, the Packers' winning ways continued well into the 1940s. In 1944, the 31-year-old receiver led the league with 58 receptions from new quarterback Irv Comp. Hutson also led the NFL with 866 receiving yards and nine touchdowns as Green Bay returned to the title game.

As it turned out, the Packers faced their former quarterback. With several NFL players away serving in World War II (1939–1945), the Giants lured Herber out of retirement in 1944. But neither Herber nor his former passing partner had much impact on the game. Hutson caught only two passes, though he did kick the extra point on both Green Bay touchdowns. Meanwhile, the Packers' defense intercepted Herber four times, and Green Bay won 14–7.

Hutson played one more season and then retired as the NFL's dominant receiver to date. He had caught 488 passes. No other NFL receiver had cracked 200. Hutson's record of 99 touchdown catches stood until 1989.

Throughout the last half of the 1940s, the Packers slowly fell in the standings. After back-to-back losing seasons in 1948 and 1949,

The Packers celebrate in the locker room after beating the Giants in the 1944 title game.

Packers quarterback Tobin Rote, *left*, tries to fend off a tackler in a 1955 game against the Cleveland Browns.

many wondered whether Lambeau could still coach in the NFL. By the end of the 1949 season, the Packers were losing not only on the field but also at the box office. In February 1950, Lambeau left the team he built.

Things got worse after Lambeau left. In 1958, the Packers finished 1–10–1. It was the proud franchise's 11th straight season without a winning record. Meanwhile, Green Bay remained by far the smallest city in the NFL. Even though the team had opened its new City Stadium in 1957, fans worried they might not have a team much longer.

Vince Lombardi went 89-29-4 and 9-1 in the playoffs during his nine seasons as Green Bay's head coach.

CHAPTER 3

LOMBARDI'S LEGENDS

On January 28, 1959, the Packers hired Vince Lombardi as their new head coach and general manager. He arrived from New York, where as the offensive coordinator he had helped build the Giants into a championship team. But that didn't mean people in Green Bay were familiar with their new leader.

Though Green Bay fans might not have known him, Lombardi had been successful wherever he coached. He made that very clear to his players at their first meeting. "I've never been on a losing team, gentlemen," he said, "and I do not intend to start now."

Lombardi stuck to his word. After going 1-10-1 in 1958, the Packers improved to 7-5 in Lombardi's first season. Then, before the 1960 season, Green Bay got another boost when Pete Rozelle took over as NFL commissioner.

Among his ideas for the league was that all the teams should share the NFL's profits equally. The plan ensured that professional football could survive in tiny Green Bay.

THE GOLDEN BOY

While hiring Lombardi proved key to Green Bay's success, the Packers also had a new wave of talented players coming in. On defense, young linemen Henry Jordan and Willie Davis were backed up by hard-hitting linebacker Ray Nitschke and smooth safety Willie Wood. All four players were 26 or younger in 1960. And all were on their way to Hall of Fame careers.

Intimidating linebacker Ray Nitschke, *right*, was the leader of Green Bay's punishing defense in the 1960s.

On offense, fifth-year quarterback Bart Starr passed his way to his first Pro Bowl in 1960. Many of his throws went to his favorite receiving target, Boyd Dowler. In the backfield, Jim Taylor and Paul Hornung ran behind the combination of right guard Jerry Kramer and right tackle Forrest Gregg. While Taylor rushed for more than 1,100 yards, Hornung proved to be Green Bay's most dangerous weapon. "The Golden Boy" led the league with 13 rushing touchdowns. He also caught 28 passes and kicked 15 field goals. With 176 points scored that season, Hornung set an NFL record.

Packers quarterback Bart Starr was named the NFL's MVP in 1966.

After going 8–4, the Packers reached the 1960 NFL Championship Game but lost a close game to the Philadelphia Eagles. In 1961, a more experienced Green Bay team finished 11–3. Hornung won the league Most Valuable Player (MVP) Award after leading the NFL with 146 points. This time, the Packers faced the Giants in the title game.

Packers running back Paul Hornung scored 50 rushing touchdowns, 12 receiving touchdowns, and five passing touchdowns in his career.

Hornung opened the scoring in the second quarter when he ran for a 6-yard touchdown and then kicked the extra point. He was just getting started. With three more field goals and three more extra points, Hornung totaled 19 points. That set a record for a single player in the title game. His standout performance led the Packers to a 37–0 win and their first championship in 17 years.

THE PACKER SWEEP

Having finally reached the top of the mountain, Lombardi intended to stay there. The Packers' coach was known for his inspirational sayings. One of his most famous was "Winning is not a sometime thing; it's an all-the-time thing."

> ***"WINNING IS NOT A SOMETIME THING; IT'S AN ALL-THE-TIME THING."***
>
> ***—VINCE LOMBARDI***

The 1962 Packers came close to perfection. The team rolled to a 13–1 record while scoring the most points of any team on offense and giving up the fewest points on defense. Green Bay became known for running the Power Sweep, a run play that called for both guards to pull to one side of the field. There, they tried to create an open lane for the running back. The team made the play so famous that many called it the Packer Sweep. With that play at the center of the offense, Taylor piled up league-leading totals of 1,474 yards and 19 touchdowns.

Taylor continued his charge in the NFL title game. Facing the Giants again on a bitterly cold day in New York, the rugged fullback fought through hard hits all game on 31 punishing carries for 85 yards. He finished the day with a gashed elbow, a cut tongue, and the Packers' only touchdown in a 16–7 victory to clinch another title.

THE NFL'S FINEST

Though the Packers remained a powerful team in 1963 and 1964, they fell short of the division title both years. One big reason was the loss of Hornung, whom the NFL suspended for the entire 1963 season for gambling on games. When he returned, persistent knee injuries often turned him into a shell of his former self. But Hornung was at his best during Week 13 of the 1965 season as the Packers defeated the Baltimore Colts 42–27. Hornung scored three rushing touchdowns and also caught 50- and 65-yard touchdown passes from Starr.

Green Bay finished 10–3–1, tied with Baltimore for the best record in the division. The teams needed a one-game playoff to decide who went to the NFL Championship Game. After falling behind 10–0, Green Bay got back into the game on a 1-yard touchdown run by Hornung in the third quarter. Still down 10–7 late in the fourth, Green Bay lined up for a game-tying 22-yard field-goal attempt from kicker Don Chandler. The kick went high above the upright and appeared to miss wide. But the officials called the kick good. The Packers won on a 25-yard kick from Chandler in overtime. A week later, they knocked off the Cleveland Browns 23–12 to win their third championship of the decade.

LAMBEAU FIELD

Curly Lambeau died before the 1965 season. Though he had left the team on poor terms nearly two decades earlier, the Packers made sure to honor the man who had founded the team. Before the season, Green Bay renamed City Stadium as Lambeau Field.

The Packers take on the Houston Texans in the snow at Lambeau Field in 2016.

SUPER BOWL BOUND

The 1965 NFL Championship Game was the last of its kind. The upstart American Football League (AFL) arrived in 1960 in hopes of challenging the NFL. By the start of the 1966 season, the two leagues had

Green Bay defensive linemen Willie Davis (87) and Henry Jordan (74) sandwich Kansas City Chiefs quarterback Len Dawson in Super Bowl I.

decided to merge. As part of the deal, the leagues established an end-of-season championship game. Though it was called the AFL-NFL World Championship when it was first played on January 15, 1967, it soon became known as the Super Bowl.

After finishing 12–2 in 1966, Green Bay held off the Dallas Cowboys 34–27 on a last-second interception in the NFL title game. That sent the Packers to the first Super Bowl, where they faced the AFL champion Kansas City Chiefs. It was a tough spot for Green Bay. Almost everyone considered the NFL to be a superior league.

Green Bay took the field knowing a win would back up that idea. But a loss would be considered an embarrassing upset.

Things got worse for Lombardi in the first quarter when Dowler went down with a shoulder injury. His backup, Max McGee, was a 35-year-old veteran. Since he didn't expect to play, McGee had broken team rules and stayed out very late the night before. He was still worn out when he had to go into the game.

Wide receiver Max McGee caught only four passes during the 1966 regular season. He finished Super Bowl I with seven catches for 138 yards and two touchdowns.

Late in the first quarter with the game still scoreless, Starr took the snap at the Kansas City 37. Spotting McGee open down the middle, the Packers' quarterback fired a pass to his veteran receiver. The ball was behind McGee, but he reached back and made a bobbling catch before outracing the Kansas City defense into the end zone. The first touchdown in Super Bowl history was scored by a player who didn't expect to be on the field.

Green Bay led 14–10 at halftime. Then the defense came up big early in the third quarter. Wood picked off a pass from Kansas City quarterback Len Dawson on the Chiefs' first drive and raced 50 yards to the Kansas City 5. Green Bay running back Elijah Pitts blasted up the middle on the next play for a touchdown.

From there, the Packers wore down the Chiefs with a punishing ground attack. Green Bay won 35–10. The team's dynasty of the 1960s appeared unstoppable.

Elijah Pitts, *center*, scored two touchdowns in the second half of Super Bowl I.

THE ICE BOWL

The Packers and Cowboys squared off again for the 1967 NFL title. In addition to battling each other, they had to fight it out with brutally cold temperatures on New Year's Eve in Green Bay. At game time, the thermometer read minus-13 degrees Fahrenheit (minus-25° C). The game became known as "the Ice Bowl."

Through a constant cloud of breath from the players, the teams hammered each other all afternoon. With less than five minutes to go, Dallas took a 17–14 lead. Starr guided the Packers down the field to the Dallas 1 with under a minute to play, but the Cowboys stuffed two attempts at the end zone. Starr called Green Bay's last timeout with 16 seconds to go.

Instead of kicking a field goal to force overtime, Lombardi and Starr decided to gamble for the win. Starr took the snap and plunged forward behind Kramer and center Ken Bowman. The veteran quarterback just barely sneaked over the goal line. The Packers survived the cold and the Cowboys for a 21–17 victory and a spot in Super Bowl II.

FOR THE OLD MAN

Facing the Oakland Raiders in the Super Bowl, Green Bay built a 16–7 halftime lead. However, the Packers felt as though they had played sloppy football. Their beloved head coach had taught them better than that. And many wondered whether they were playing their last game for Lombardi.

Rumors had swirled for months that this was the 54-year-old coach's last season. But no one knew for sure. In the locker room at

The official signals touchdown after Packers quarterback Bart Starr (15) dived over the goal line with seconds to go to win "the Ice Bowl" for Green Bay on December 31, 1967.

Packers cornerback Herb Adderley looks up the field after pulling in his key interception in Super Bowl II.

halftime, the Packers weren't taking any chances. If Lombardi was done, they wanted to send him out properly. They wanted to win it "for the old man," said Kramer.

A rushing touchdown by running back Donny Anderson and a field goal by Chandler pushed Green Bay's lead to 26-7 in the fourth quarter. Then cornerback Herb Adderley put the game away. The future Hall of Famer had joined the Packers in 1961 and quickly established himself as an expert thief. He had recorded at least four interceptions every year since 1962.

Oakland quarterback Daryle Lamonica dropped back and heaved a pass down the right sideline. Adderley hurled himself in front of the Raiders' receiver and intercepted the pass at the Green Bay 40. He then raced down the field, slowing only to brush Lamonica aside at the Oakland 15 on the way to the end zone.

The Packers won 33–14. In what indeed proved to be Lombardi's last game with Green Bay, his players carried him off the field. Over his nine seasons, the Packers had won five championships, including the first two Super Bowls. In 1970, the trophy given out to the Super Bowl winner was renamed the Vince Lombardi Trophy.

Green Bay coach Vince Lombardi gets a ride off the field after Super Bowl II, his final game in charge of the Packers.

As it turned out, many of the team's aging stars followed Lombardi out the door. The Packers fell to 6–7–1 the next year. Little did anyone in Green Bay know how long it would take to return to the top.

Receiver James Lofton was one of the few bright spots for the Packers in the 1970s and 1980s. He set team records of 530 receptions and 9,656 yards between 1978 and 1986.

CHAPTER 4

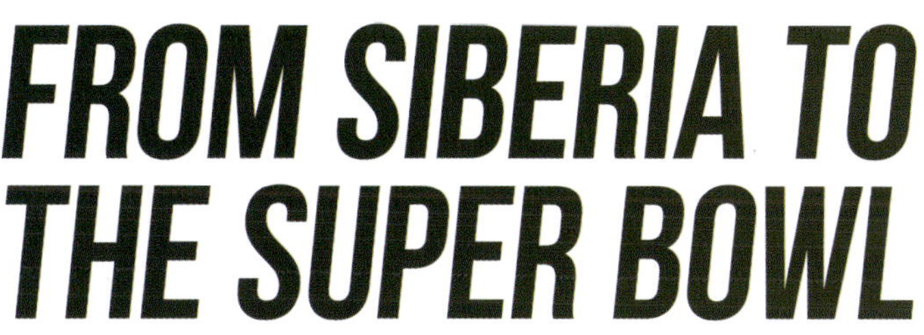

FROM SIBERIA TO THE SUPER BOWL

AS THE PACKERS PUT TOGETHER THEIR INCREDIBLE DYNASTY IN THE 1960s, many fans began referring to Green Bay as "Titletown." But in the 1970s and 1980s, the team drifted aimlessly. During those decades, Green Bay won just two division titles and a single playoff game while posting only three winning records. Opponents were no longer intimidated to play in Titletown. Instead, many around the league joked about Green Bay as "the NFL's Siberia," referring to the frigid province in Russia where that nation exiled many prisoners.

In 1991, new team president Bob Harlan tried to shake the Packers out of their slumber. He hired Ron Wolf as the team's general manager. Wolf had been a respected NFL scout since the early 1960s, mainly for the successful Oakland/ Los Angeles Raiders.

Defensive end Reggie White recorded 68 1/2 sacks in six seasons with the Packers.

Wolf's first big move was hiring San Francisco 49ers offensive coordinator Mike Holmgren as Green Bay's head coach. Holmgren had been an assistant on three Super Bowl winners. He was known as a good teacher and a creative play caller.

Wolf also made a pair of on-field moves that steered the Packers back to the top. Few paid much attention when the team traded for Brett Favre in 1992. The quarterback had played college football out of the limelight at Southern Mississippi. He then spent one year as a backup for the Atlanta Falcons. When Favre arrived in Green Bay, most fans simply wondered how to pronounce his last name (it rhymes with *carve*).

Quarterback Brett Favre led the NFL in passing yards twice and in touchdowns four times during his 16 seasons with the Packers.

Wolf turned a lot more heads before the next season when he signed All-Pro defensive end Reggie White to bolster Green Bay's defense. White was known as "the Minister of Defense" for both his work as a preacher and his punishment of NFL quarterbacks while with the Philadelphia Eagles. Behind the two future Hall of Famers, the future suddenly looked brighter in Green Bay.

GUNSLINGER

The fun-loving, hard-throwing Favre quickly became one of the league's most exciting players. Many of his teammates complained of bruised palms or even broken fingers after trying to catch Favre's rocket passes. Because of his arm strength and unwillingness to give up on a play, Favre often forced throws into tight spaces. It didn't always work. Favre eventually threw more interceptions than any other quarterback in NFL history. But he also managed to pull off incredible feats on a weekly basis. And soon the Packers were back in contention.

Holmgren, Favre, and White led Green Bay back to the playoffs as a wild-card team in 1993 and 1994. Both years, Green Bay lost in the divisional round. After a division title in the 1995 season and an MVP season from Favre, the Packers advanced to the conference title game before falling to the Dallas Cowboys. By the start of the 1996 season, Green Bay fans were hopeful that their team was about to take the leap back to championship status.

A GRAND RETURN

In 1996, the Packers could seemingly do anything. Behind Favre's NFL-best 39 touchdown passes, Green Bay averaged the most points in the league. Though White had one of his less productive seasons with 8 1/2 sacks, the 35-year-old lineman provided strong leadership for the league's best defense. In the secondary, All-Pro safety LeRoy Butler snagged five interceptions.

The Packers were also dangerous on special teams. Before the season, Wolf signed receiver/kick returner

Mike Holmgren went 75–37 as Green Bay's head coach from 1992 to 1998.

Desmond Howard. The 5-foot-10-inch, 185-pound Howard had won the Heisman Trophy as college football's best player in 1991. He struggled in the NFL as a receiver, but his blazing speed and cat-quick moves made him a stellar return man. In 1996, he brought back three punts for touchdowns and averaged more than 20 yards per kickoff return.

The Packers finished 13–3, often blowing away opponents. Only two of their wins were decided by a touchdown or less. Playing in front of raucous crowds in Green Bay, the Packers kept rolling in the postseason. Just minutes into their playoff opener against the 49ers, Howard caught a punt at his own 29. Starting to his right, he

Green Bay running back Edgar Bennett (34) charges forward with the ball during the Packers' playoff win over the San Francisco 49ers in January 1997.

broke back up the middle of the field, dancing his way through five would-be tacklers before breaking free for a 71-yard score. Green Bay rolled to a 35–14 win.

A week later, Favre threw for 292 yards and a pair of touchdowns in the National Football Conference (NFC) title game against the Carolina Panthers. Running backs Dorsey Levens and Edgar Bennett combined for nearly 200 yards rushing. Green Bay once again pulled away for a 30–13 win. For the first time in nearly three decades, the Packers were back in the Super Bowl.

By the time the Packers arrived in New Orleans for Super Bowl XXXI, Favre was well known to football fans for his enthusiasm on the field. But early in the game against the New England Patriots, he got a chance to show a worldwide audience how much he loved his job. Green Bay took over at its own 45 with 12:19 to go in the first quarter. On the team's second play, Favre dropped

THE LAMBEAU LEAP

On December 26, 1993, the Packers hosted the Los Angeles Raiders. Early in the fourth quarter, Green Bay safety LeRoy Butler scooped up a fumble and ran 21 yards for a touchdown. He celebrated by jumping into the stands behind the end zone. Butler's celebration kicked off a new Green Bay tradition. The team's players still celebrate home touchdowns by launching themselves into the waiting arms of fans. The celebration is known as "the Lambeau Leap."

Safety LeRoy Butler does "the Lambeau Leap" after scoring a touchdown in December 1995.

back and spotted receiver Andre Rison free down the middle of the field. Favre lofted a deep pass that hit his receiver in stride. As Rison raced to the end zone, Favre ripped off his helmet and held it high above his head. He sprinted to the Green Bay sideline with a beaming smile on his face.

Favre sprints to the sideline after throwing his early touchdown pass to Andre Rison in Super Bowl XXXI.

Packers fans everywhere were glowing when Favre dropped back early in the second quarter and lofted another deep ball to Antonio Freeman. The receiver sprinted down the sideline for an 81-yard score, and the Packers led 17–14. Favre later raced left for a 2-yard touchdown run to give Green Bay a 27–14 halftime lead. But the underdog Patriots hung around. In the third quarter, New England star rusher Curtis Martin scored from 18 yards out. The extra point cut Green Bay's lead to six.

All game, Howard had been threatening to break a long return. After a 31-yard punt return early in the game, he popped up and got into a verbal spat with the Patriots who had tackled him. Howard never stopped talking to his opponents after that, but on the kickoff after Martin's touchdown, he let his play speak for itself. Howard fielded the kick at Green Bay's 1-yard line and took off up the middle, following strong blocks from his teammates. Only one

Patriot had a shot at Howard, near the 30-yard line. The speedy returner bounced off the hit and barely broke stride. He sprinted past New England kicker Adam Vinatieri and into the Super Bowl record book with a 99-yard touchdown return.

> **"I KNEW THAT SOONER OR LATER I WAS GOING TO SCORCH 'EM."**
>
> **—DESMOND HOWARD**

"I knew that sooner or later I was going to scorch 'em," Howard said after the game.

Even with a quarter to play, Howard's return all but sealed the Packers' victory. Green Bay added a two-point conversion to go up 35–21. That proved to be the final score as the Packers claimed their third Super Bowl championship.

IRON MAN

Favre won his third straight MVP Award in 1997 and led the Packers back to the Super Bowl against the Denver Broncos. Though Green Bay came into the game as heavy favorites, the Broncos stayed with the Packers all game and took a 31–24 lead with 1:47 remaining. Favre had a chance to lead a game-tying drive, but after he completed his first four passes, the Broncos forced three straight incompletions to thwart the drive and secure the title.

One of the toughest players to ever put on an NFL uniform, Favre frequently battled through aches and pains. He never missed a game well into the 2000s. But after he began hinting at retirement early in the decade, the Packers started to plan for life after their superstar was gone. In 2005, they drafted quarterback Aaron Rodgers in the first round of the draft. However, Favre played three more years in Green Bay, which sometimes created an awkward situation between the two players.

Favre started 275 consecutive games for the Packers between 1992 and 2007. At the time, no other quarterback had started more than 200 in a row.

Favre seemingly retired after the 2007 season, only to change his mind in the summer of 2008. By that point, the Packers were ready to move on. They traded Favre to the New York Jets. It was an unceremonious ending for one of the franchise's greatest icons. But in Green Bay, another superstar was ready to take over.

Quarterback Aaron Rodgers led the Packers to winning seasons every year from 2009 to 2017.

TITLETOWN

AARON RODGERS DROPPED BACK TO PASS AND QUICKLY BEGAN READING the Arizona Cardinals' defense. The Packers and Cardinals were tied 45–45 in overtime of their wild-card playoff game in January 2010. It was already the highest-scoring playoff game in NFL history. Rodgers had thrown four touchdown passes and rushed for another in his first career playoff game. This time, as Rodgers cocked his arm to throw, an Arizona defender knocked the ball loose. Arizona linebacker Karlos Dansby caught it out of the air and raced 17 yards for the winning score. The Packers' season was over.

The bitter defeat didn't shake the Packers' confidence that they could be a championship team. The Super Bowl after the 2010 season was scheduled to be played in Dallas. Before training camp in the summer, Rodgers bought Texas-style

Mike McCarthy, *right*, won 125 games as Green Bay's head coach between 2006 and 2018. Only Curly Lambeau coached the team to more victories.

cowboy hats and bolo ties for several teammates. Head coach Mike McCarthy felt the same confidence. Photos from Green Bay's storied past draped the team's meeting room. McCarthy placed an empty frame in the corner of the room and told his team their picture would hang there after the season.

CHAMPIONSHIP BELTS

The Packers had reason to be confident. In Rodgers's two years as Green Bay's starter, he had erased any fears that the Packers would struggle to replace the legendary Brett Favre. Rodgers had an accurate arm and a knack for big plays late in games. He also manipulated defenses in clever ways. One of his favorite tricks was using a hard snap count to draw defenders offside. As soon as he saw the flag come out, Rodgers knew he had a free play. He would then launch the ball deep, hoping for a big gain.

Rodgers formed a strong connection with Pro Bowl receiver Greg Jennings and veteran fan favorite Donald Driver. On defense, safety Nick Collins and cornerbacks Charles Woodson and Tramon Williams made the Packers tough to throw against. But the team's biggest defensive playmaker was pass-rushing linebacker Clay Matthews. Fans could easily spot the talkative Matthews due to his long blond hair flowing out from under his helmet as he terrorized quarterbacks all season.

The Packers picked wide receiver Donald Driver, *right*, in the seventh round of the 1999 draft. He retired in 2012 as the team's all-time leader in receptions and receiving yards.

Despite the Packers' talent and confidence, the 2010 regular season didn't go as planned. Fifteen players landed on injured reserve, which ended their seasons. Even Rodgers missed a key late-season matchup with the New England Patriots after suffering a concussion the week before.

Green Bay linebacker Clay Matthews had 13 1/2 sacks during the 2010 season.

Green Bay lost to New England. With two games to go, the team held an 8–6 record. The Packers needed wins in their last two games or they would miss the playoffs. Rodgers returned in Week 16 and threw for 404 yards and four touchdowns in a 45–17 demolition of the New York Giants. A week later, he lofted a 1-yard touchdown pass to tight end Donald Lee early in the fourth quarter against the Chicago Bears. The score broke a 3–3 tie, and the Packers hung on for the playoff-clinching victory.

Green Bay running back James Jones tries to break through a pair of tacklers during a playoff game against the Atlanta Falcons in January 2011.

Rodgers kept his strong play going in the playoffs. He tossed six touchdown passes in road wins over the Philadelphia Eagles and Atlanta Falcons. Many of his touchdowns were punctuated by the team's signature celebration. After big plays, Rodgers and his teammates would mime wrapping wrestling championship belts around their waists.

Green Bay traveled south to face the Bears in the NFC Championship Game. It was the first postseason meeting ever between the two storied rivals. Both teams struggled on offense, but Green Bay defensive tackle B. J. Raji came up with a big play in the fourth quarter. With the Packers up 14–7 and just over six minutes to play, Raji dropped off the line and intercepted Chicago's Caleb Hanie at the Chicago 18. The 334-pound lineman then rumbled to the end zone for the key score in a 21–14 victory.

THE WAITING LIST

Since 1960, every game at City Stadium/ Lambeau Field has been sold out. The team estimates that the waiting list for season tickets is roughly 147,000 names long. And since so few people give up their tickets, many fans have waited decades for their chance to purchase seats at Lambeau. Other fans have passed their season tickets on to relatives in their wills.

Green Bay fans are often called "cheeseheads." Many wear hats shaped like wedges of cheese to games.

A LEGACY MOMENT

The Packers faced another historic team in Super Bowl XLV. The Pittsburgh Steelers were bidding for their seventh Super Bowl title. Rodgers and the Packers jumped out to a 21–3 first-half lead on two touchdown passes and a 37-yard interception return by Collins. But the big lead didn't last. As the fourth quarter opened, Green Bay led just 21–17. And the Steelers were on the move.

It had been a quiet game for Matthews, with just two tackles. But the team's

Packers cornerback Sam Shields, *top*, jumps on B. J. Raji's back after Raji scored his 18-yard interception return against the Chicago Bears in the NFC title game on January 23, 2011.

defensive leader stepped up when his team needed him most. On second-and-two from the Green Bay 33, Matthews slammed into Pittsburgh running back Rashard Mendenhall in the backfield.

The hit jarred the ball loose, and Green Bay linebacker Desmond Bishop fell on it. Eight plays later, Rodgers took a shotgun snap and fired a perfect spiral to a wide-open Jennings in the corner of the end zone. Green Bay went up 28–17 after the extra point.

Wide receiver Greg Jennings makes a leaping touchdown catch in the fourth quarter of Super Bowl XLV.

Though Pittsburgh mounted another late rally, Green Bay still held a 31–25 lead in the final seconds. On fourth-and-five, the Packers' defense snuffed out Pittsburgh's final drive by breaking up a pass with 56 seconds left, and the Packers' sideline exploded with joy. The smallest city in the NFL was on top of the league once again. McCarthy said after the season, "They never lost sight of the goal. They always believed."

CLOSE CALLS

After winning the Super Bowl, the Packers looked set up for another dynasty. Rodgers won the MVP Award in 2011 as he guided Green Bay to a 13–0 start. But the Kansas City Chiefs derailed Green Bay's perfect season in the next game. And in the divisional round of the playoffs, the underdog Giants shocked the Packers 37–20.

Green Bay followed a similar pattern for the rest of the decade. Rodgers played brilliantly, and the Packers were seemingly always in contention. But the team suffered several bitter playoff defeats. In 2014, after another MVP season from Rodgers, the Packers marched to the NFC title game. With just over two minutes to go, they led the defending Super Bowl champion Seattle Seahawks 19–7. But Green Bay gave up two touchdowns in less than 40 seconds to fall behind. Despite tying the game on a last-second field goal, the Packers lost 28–22 in overtime. A year later in the divisional round, the Packers trailed the Cardinals by a touchdown late. Rodgers heaved a last-second 41-yard Hail Mary to reserve receiver Jeff Janis to force overtime as time expired. However, the Cardinals won 26–20 in the extra session.

Packers receiver Jeff Janis, *bottom*, holds up the ball after his Hail Mary reception against the Arizona Cardinals in January 2016.

A NEW LOVE

Between the 2016 and 2020 seasons, the Packers reached the NFC Championship Game three times. They lost all three. By the end of the 2020 season, Rodgers, then 37 years old, had grown frustrated. He hoped the team would draft another offensive weapon to get Green Bay over the hump. But in the draft's first round, the team instead picked quarterback Jordan Love. Suddenly, Rodgers was in the same situation he had been in 15 years earlier with Brett Favre. Only this time, Rodgers was the veteran.

He didn't give up his spot easily. Rodgers earned MVP honors for a third time in 2020. He won the award again in 2021 as Love watched from the sideline. In those two seasons, Rodgers threw 85 touchdown passes and only nine interceptions. But even that brilliance couldn't get Green Bay back to the top. After the 2020 Packers fell in the NFC title game, the 2021 Packers lost their playoff opener. Green Bay missed the playoffs altogether

The Packers hired Matt LaFleur to be the team's head coach on January 8, 2019.

Wide receiver Davante Adams makes a leaping catch against the Cleveland Browns in 2021. Adams set a Packers record with 123 receptions that season.

in 2022. The team decided to move on. Just as they had done with Favre, the Packers traded Rodgers to the New York Jets.

Love started slowly in 2023, but his confidence grew as the season went on. After his late game-winning touchdown against the Los Angeles Chargers in Week 11, Love and the Packers took off. Connecting with young receivers Romeo Doubs, Jayden Reed, and Christian Watson, Love led Green Bay back to the playoffs.

PACKERS TROPHY CASE

SUPER BOWL CHAMPIONSHIPS: 4

Super Bowl I – January 15, 1967
Super Bowl II – January 15, 1968
Super Bowl XXXI – January 26, 1997
Super Bowl XLV – February 6, 2011

NFL CHAMPIONSHIPS: 11

1929, 1930, 1931, 1935, 1939, 1944, 1961, 1962, 1965, 1966, 1967

CONFERENCE CHAMPIONSHIPS: 3

1996, 1997, 2010

DIVISION TITLES: 28

NFL West: 1935, 1938, 1939, 1941, 1944, 1960, 1961, 1962, 1965, 1966
NFL Central: 1967
NFC Central: 1972, 1982, 1995, 1996, 1997
NFC North: 2002, 2003, 2004, 2007, 2011, 2012, 2013, 2014, 2016, 2019, 2020, 2021

Opening on the road in Dallas, Love carved up the Cowboys' defense. Green Bay charged to a 27–0 lead before ultimately winning 48–32.

Though the Packers' playoff run ended the next week, Love had shown he could continue the team's great quarterback tradition. Then he backed it up by leading Green Bay back to the postseason in 2024. It was the team's 14th playoff appearance in 18 seasons. The next step for Green Bay was returning to the Super Bowl and adding another championship. With Love at the helm, Packers fans had hope that the team would soon be writing the next proud chapter in its storied history.

Packers quarterback Jordan Love, *right*, celebrates with receiver Jayden Reed after a touchdown against the New York Giants in December 2023.

TIMELINE

The Packers are founded by player/coach Curly Lambeau and newspaper writer George Whitney Calhoun.

1919

1929

Green Bay wins the first of three straight NFL titles.

Led by groundbreaking receiver Don Hutson, the Packers defeat Boston 21–6 in the NFL Championship Game.

1936

1944

The Packers win the NFL title for the third time in eight years and the last time under Curly Lambeau.

Green Bay routs the New York Giants 37–0 for the team's first title under new coach Vince Lombardi.

1961

1966

The Packers defeat the Cleveland Browns 23–12 on January 2 to win their third championship of the decade.

The Packers win Super Bowl I 35–10 over the Kansas City Chiefs on January 15.

1967

1968
In Lombardi's last game as head coach, Green Bay routs the Oakland Raiders 33–14 in Super Bowl II on January 14.

The Packers trade for quarterback Brett Favre.
1992

1997
Spurred by Favre and kick returner Desmond Howard, the Packers beat the New England Patriots 35–21 in Super Bowl XXXI on January 26.

Favre plays his final game with the Packers.
2008

2011
Quarterback Aaron Rodgers leads Green Bay to a 31–25 victory over the Pittsburgh Steelers in Super Bowl XLV on February 6.

Rodgers wins the NFL MVP Award for the fourth time.
2021

2023
First-year starting quarterback Jordan Love leads the Packers to the playoffs.

GLOSSARY

amateur—a person who plays a sport without getting paid.

coordinator—an assistant coach who is in charge of the offense, defense, or special teams.

draft—a system that allows teams to acquire new players coming into the league.

exile—to be sent away as a punishment.

franchise—an entire sports organization.

fumble—losing the ball and allowing the opponent a chance to recover it.

general manager—an executive who runs a team and is responsible for finding and signing players.

Hail Mary—a long pass that has a small chance of succeeding, usually made near the end of a game as a last-ditch effort to score.

icon—a player who is well known for excellence.

merge—join with another to create something new, such as a company, a team, or a league.

Pro Bowl—a postseason competition that the NFL's all-stars are invited to compete in.

professional—involving players who are paid to perform.

retire—to end one's career.

rival—an opponent with whom a player or team has a fierce and ongoing competition.

sack–a tackle of the quarterback behind the line of scrimmage before he can pass the ball.

scandal–an action or event regarded as morally or legally wrong and causing general public outrage.

snap– the start of each play, when the center hikes the ball between his legs to a player behind him, usually the quarterback.

stock–a share of ownership in something, such as a company.

underdog–the person or team that is not expected to win.

veteran–someone who has played for many years.

will–a legal document expressing a person's wishes for their property after their death.

ONLINE RESOURCES

To learn more about the Green Bay Packers, please visit **abdobooklinks.com** or scan this QR code. These links are routinely monitored and updated to provide the most current information available.

INDEX